T0380888

BEARING PRECIOUS SEED

WENDY JONES

WestBow Press books may be ordered through booksellers or by contacting:

WestBow Press
A Division of Thomas Nelson & Zondervan
1663 Liberty Drive
Bloomington, IN 47403
www.westbowpress.com
844-714-3454

Scripture taken from the King James Version of the Bible.

ISBN: 978-1-6642-9903-0 (sc)
ISBN: 978-1-6642-9904-7 (hc)
ISBN: 978-1-6642-9905-4 (e)

Library of Congress Control Number: 2023908064

Print information available on the last page.

WestBow Press rev. date: 08/16/2023

WINNING
CHRIST

TO KNOW HIM

Yea doubtless, and I count all things but loss for the excellency of the
knowledge of Christ Jesus my Lord … That I may know him …
—Philippians 3:8, 10

When we become acquainted with God,
    our hearts will never divide with any other object.
When we become acquainted with God's purposes,
    we find that His plans are different from our own.
When we become acquainted with God's righteousness,
    we can no longer look at ourselves.
When we become acquainted with God's truth,
    we find that it requires our all.
When we become acquainted with God's ways,
    we find our feet untrained and needing a Guide.
When we become acquainted with God's light,
    we can no longer bear the shadows which all else is.
When we become acquainted with God's voice,
    our ears ever wait and listen for it above
    earth's clamor.
When we become acquainted with God's touch,
    our words and deeds will no longer move to
    murmur or condemn.
When we become acquainted with God's love,
    we find that all fears have fled away!

HIS LOVE

HIS LOVE consumes the oceans.
HIS LOVE rides every wave.
HIS LOVE pours out a bloody stream.
    Men's wicked lives to save.

HIS LOVE is stronger than sunshine,
More abundant than rain;
And though His heart's been broken,
    HIS LOVE yet remains.

HIS LOVE exceeds the universe
And enters a man of clay;
And with each breath I breathe, I say,
    "Let me give the love You gave."

I WALKED ALONE WITH GOD

And Enoch walked with God: and … God took him.
—Genesis 5:24

I WALKED alone with God
       where only the grasses grow …
       where only the trees stand tall and strong,
       where only the waters flow.

YES, WE were there a'walking
       where the little winds blow free …
       where the mountains rise against the sky,
       and no mortal eye doth see.

NOR DOTH mortal tongue
       resound in noisome tone …
       nor haughty head upheld …
       lay claim upon His throne.

BUT FAR from the strife of fools
       God's great domain did lie …
       in glory and in beauty …
       He reigns there from on high.

A SWEETNESS filled the air,
          unknown to passersby …
          as we walked alone together …
          the LORD of the earth and I!

ALLEGORY OF A FEATHER

And there shall be a time of trouble, such as never was since
there was a nation … and at that time thy people shall be
delivered, every one that shall be found written in the book.
—Daniel 12:1

Many shall be purified, and made white, and tried …
—Daniel 12:10

And they that be wise shall shine as the brightness of the firmament;
and they that turn many to righteousness as the stars for ever and ever.
—Daniel 12:3

While looking out one morning … bright …
the earth looked bare … so cold … not right …
But then I spied a feather … white …
so pure and lovely to my sight.

So special to me … in the midst of that sea
of barrenness … waste and depravity …
And as I searched for what more I could see …
I discovered new meaning … revealed to me.

For with a start I felt God speak … to my heart,
"Look closer … Child … you'll see My part.
My eyes search the earth to and fro … like a dart
for just one who will love Me … with all of his heart.

"It's such a hard task … and when I find him at last
I make him My chosen … from this world … so vast
He's whiter than any feather could pass
upon a world of sin ravaged grass."

I cried out … "Lord … here is one! … Take me! …
I'm Yours! … for now and eternity! …
And each time You search this vicinity …
You'll find this 'white feather,' Lord … waiting for Thee!"

IT IS I!

IT IS I!
Who makes the wind to blow.
IT IS I!
Who sends and melts the snow.
IT IS I!
Who makes the flower grow.
IT IS I!
Who makes the rivers flow.
IT IS I!
Who gives a smile its glow.
IT IS I!
Your human mind can't show.
IT IS I!
In Whose strength you go.
IT IS I!
Whose Word runs to and fro.
IT IS I!
Who comes to lift the low.
IT IS I!
Whose love will not bend or bow.
IT IS I!
Upon Whom your burdens throw.
IT IS I!
Who triumphs o'er every foe.
IT IS I!
With a yes for every no.
IT IS I!
Who quickens the seeds you sow.
IT IS I!
Who cares from your head to your toe.
IT IS I!
Who to anger is very slow.
IT IS I!
Who alone can free you from woe.
And IT IS I!
Whom your soul is longing to know!

SNOWFLAKES

If I wash myself with snow water, and make my hands never so clean; Yet shalt thou plunge me in the ditch, and mine own clothes shall abhor me.
—Job 9:30–31

For by one offering he hath perfected for ever them that are sanctified.
—Hebrews 10:14

Snow falling softly ... Glorious sight ...
Covering earth's dirty surface with white ...

For a moment ... I behold ... the art of God's Hand,
not yet corrupted by the touch of man.

I watch my barren world become ... purely defined,
and an idea of wonder ... overcomes my mind.

God ... why don't You cover the earth with snow?
Beneath ... even the blackest sin can't show.

In this frozen delight … seeds of evil can't grow.
Why not Lord … why not let it snow?

The snow now seemed whiter than ever before.
I was so happy … as it buried earth's floor …

But there, in the midst of my fantasy,
God interrupted … with an answer for me …

I could cover the earth with a blanket of snow
and hide a land of sin.
But all of the snow in the heavens above …
couldn't cover the hearts of men.

Their wickedness calls for … sweat … and blood … so because of
    My love for them …
My glorious Son became despicable flesh … and with hate …
    they crucified Him.

Now His blood … alone … is your answer … Child …
    if your heart will ever be free …
for I can't cover My creation with snow …
    I must wash it … with blood … thoroughly.

THE RAIN GAME

My doctrine shall drop as the rain.
—Deuteronomy 32:2

A drop of rain … he fell with pride
      As he looked out over … the countryside;

    And when he viewed the rolling fields of wheat,
He thought to himself, *I just can't be beat.*

My presence gives life to the grains and goods
    That keep the world spinning around.
    I quench folks' thirst … cool the air …
And water their barren ground.

The earth sings out with joyful glee
    Each time I start to fall;
    And if it weren't for me, there just
Wouldn't be … any life at all!

Now, as he reveled in selfish thought
    And welled up from the bliss;
    His vision was shortened, and his foolish mind
Never realized … there was one thing he'd missed …

For all around him … above him … below him,
    Millions of raindrops were falling,
    Helping each other to fulfill the task
Of refreshing the ground that was calling.

This one never observed the unity of the rain
    Or all the help he received …
    And if he'd been left to fall on his own,
He'd have never been noticed or seen!

A DRINK OF WATER

Then shall the righteous answer him, saying, Lord, when saw we thee
an hungred, and fed thee? or thirsty, and gave thee drink? … And the
King shall answer and say unto them … Inasmuch as ye have done it
unto one of the least of these my brethren, ye have done it unto me.
—Matthew 25:37, 40

I saw him in the street today;
    His face was marred with pain.
Worn-out clothes offered little relief
    From the cold and driving rain.
All caught up in my worthless affairs,
    My heart was broken in two.
While I pitied myself over careless mishaps,
    Living was all he could do;

And as he passed with face 'void of joy,
    Shame burned my eyes with tears.
When Jesus said, "I'm the least of these.
    Can I have just a drink of water?"

I saw him try to make his way—
    A wheelchair for his feet.
He rolled amidst a mocking world—
    His enemy—the street.
I saw a head wanting to be held high,
    A heart that didn't want to die,
A mind that questioned and wondered why,
    Feelings that felt, and rejected eyes.
Again my heart was touched by God.
    I heard my Master say,
"I need just a drink of water;
    Could you spare Me a glass today?"
I see him now on every street.
    My heart fills to the brim.
I ask the Lord with pleading prayers
    To give of His mercy to him.
He answers me ever faithfully,
    Saying, "You are the mercy I give,
And, again, I say, give Me a drink
    Of waters that make one live."

Lord, let me be the servant of all.
    Release Your love and life
To flow from me so full and free,
    Giving to all Your Light.
Take all my strength and life to be
    Broken bread to feed Your hungry!
And let me never fail to offer my Lord …
    A glass of living water.

JESUS PRAYING AT NIGHT

And he cometh unto the disciples, and findeth them asleep, and
saith unto Peter, What, could ye not watch with me one hour?
—Matthew 26:40

Oh, earth, keep silent before your King.
　　This night in your garden He doth appear.
　　　　So near your bowers will His voice ring.

There in your presence He softly sings,
　　Strains from a heart that knows not fear.
　　　　His life … a sacrifice … He brings.

The souls of the hemlock and olive do cling
　　To the words from His lips they can hear
　　　　And seal in their knotted trunks unutterable things.

The leaves tremble; the wind doth take wing;
　　The darkness must cover His falling tears;
　　　　Now drops of blood the ground do sting.

"On Thy Will, Father, Myself I fling!"
　　His tongue would melt the human ear.
　　　　From the shadows, flowers peer upon His offering.

Oh, earth, keep silent before your King
　　As He with me this night walks here.
　　　　Give foot 'neath me as I come to sing,
　　　　"On Thy Will, Father, myself I fling!"

IN BETWEEN

LET US HEAR THE CONCLUSION OF THE WHOLE MATTER:
FEAR GOD, AND KEEP HIS COMMANDMENTS: FOR THIS
IS THE WHOLE DUTY OF MAN. FOR GOD SHALL BRING
EVERY WORK INTO JUDGMENT, WITH EVERY SECRET
THING, WHETHER IT BE GOOD OR WHETHER IT BE EVIL.
—Ecclesiastes 12:13–14

Heaven's above me   The way I live
And Hell's beneath   Upon this plane
   And I'm betwixt the two.   The things I say and do.

Are all from above
Or else beneath
   Or toward them this I know.

     And which I choose
     While here I live
     Will determine which way I go.

So with eyes above
Not once below
   My heart will reach for the sky.
And if while on earth
Heaven I love,
I'll go there by and by!

THE GREAT CORONATION

LET THIS MIND BE IN YOU, WHICH WAS ALSO IN
CHRIST JESUS: WHO TOOK UPON HIM THE FORM OF
A SERVANT … AND BECAME OBEDIENT EVEN UNTO
THE DEATH OF THE CROSS. WHEREFORE GOD ALSO
HATH HIGHLY EXALTED HIM, THAT AT THE NAME OF
JESUS EVERY KNEE SHOULD BOW, AND EVERY TONGUE
SHOULD CONFESS THAT JESUS CHRIST IS LORD.
—Philippians 2:5, 7–10

The crowds were crying cruelty in the heat
    And cursing e'er the most they knew not what—
The Son of God in flesh on dragging feet
    That bore Him unto death's awaiting spot.
Tongues like bows poured arrows into the street
Of mockery and hate their hearts did clot;
    But those who laughed at Jesus's agitation
    Knew not their eyes beheld His Coronation!

Had they but known the blood they spilt had bought
> The Kingdom of our Christ forevermore;

And the work their wicked hands had wrought
> Did but entitle Him as Lord of Lords—

Their foolish jeers of "Hail! King of the Jews!"

The taunting crown of vicious, bloody thorns—
> Our Master knew they marked in that dread hour
> The actual acclamations of His power

'Twas for this moment, He had lived His life
> And in it was His Godly kingship born;

Amid' humiliation, pain, and strife
> His heart ascended to the highest throne.

Lain a sheep before the butcher's knife

The night was but the clarion of the morn.
> His Words "If you lift Me up upon this tree,
> I will surely draw all men to Me!"

IMPRESSIONS

BUT I FOLLOW AFTER, IF THAT I MAY APPREHEND THAT
FOR WHICH ALSO I AM APPREHENDED OF CHRIST JESUS.
—Philippians 3:12

He opens the door that none can shut
He shuts and none can open
 He's the first, the last, the Key of David,
 The Beginning and the End.

No greater love hath any man
Than to lay down His life for His friends:
 No greater love has this world seen
 Than the love it saw in Him.

Is the servant greater than his Master, dear?
Is he better than his Lord?
 Can he without His Master's work
 Receive His same reward?

Shall he unmocked, undiscouraged go—
When the Savior was reviled by men?
 Yet in spite of how they criticized
 The prize, He still did win!

Oh, just to know as I am known
He Who has prepared my way;
 And on that for which He's laid hold of me,
 A sacred hold to lay!

PROVERBS 22:11

He that loveth …
  Pureness of heart …
    to be desired above all
    maketh great the small
    will not let one fall.

Though the world doth depart …
    still yet we must seek
    this treasure to keep,
    knowing life we shall reap.

No other beauty could start …
    with it to compare
    its rewards are rare
    in this life and the life over there,

For the pure in heart shall see God.

JESUS SAVES

OF OLD THOU HAST LAID THE FOUNDATION OF THE
EARTH: AND THE HEAVENS ARE THE WORK OF THY HANDS.
—Psalm 102:25

Jesus saves! Why count ye it a light thing?
Earth was void … thrashing about in nothing.
Saving it, howe'er, He made it something.
Utterly formed by the power of His command
Since then He lent this small estate to man.

Screeching to its end, the earth still turns
Aware of chaos that within it churns
Vehemently … for an answer does it yearn.
Earth will be redeemed with ease by Him!
Such potency doth save the hearts of men!

IF JUST RECOGNITION WERE MADE …

IT was His blood,
                Instead of our blood
        That spilt on the ground
HIS tears,
                Not ours
        Ran mightily down
THE whip
                Cut His shoulders,
        His back was torn
HIS head,
                Not ours
        Wore the crown of thorns
HIS face was spat on,
                Smitten, and bruised;
        His holy Name horribly abused
HIS garment
                Was taken
        And gambled for
HIS arms,
                Not our arms
        The rugged cross bore

HIS heart,
　　　Not ours
　　Was broken with pain
WHEN denied
　　　By His friends
　　In the hour of shame;
AND His feet
　　　Not our feet
　　Made Calvary's climb
HIS hands
　　　Pierced with nails,
　　Not yours or mine
HIS cross, not our cross
　　　Was lifted on high
JESUS for us
　　　Was chosen to die
IT was His blood,
　　　　Instead of our blood
　　　That paid the final price;
NOW HIS LIFE,
　　　　Instead of our life …
Really is … only right.

NOT BY SIGHT

WHILE WE LOOK NOT AT THINGS WHICH ARE SEEN,
BUT AT THE THINGS WHICH ARE NOT SEEN: FOR THE
THINGS WHICH ARE SEEN ARE TEMPORAL; BUT THE
THINGS WHICH ARE NOT SEEN ARE ETERNAL.
—2 Corinthians 4:18

Close your eyes … And let arise
    the feelings brought by blindness.
Open them not … But try to spot
    the things you hear in darkness
Through that inner vision
The spirit man's been given.

Unable to survey the earth … Or look upon its mirth,
    yet knowing that it's lying all around;
And still realize … That through the black disguise
    remain the sky and trees and grass and ground.
Learn to feel and listen
'Til nothing you are missing.

So 'tis our sight … In a carnal night
    smothered by thickest dark.
Just because we can't see … There are still things that be
    in the perfect world apart;
A real and living Heaven
Unto God's sons is given.

So like this … Walk not amiss
    by sight, but by faith alone—
Seeking a land … Made without hands
    where the King sits on His throne—
As seeing Him Who invisible is
Until a holy vista to us He gives.

EVEN SO, WILL IT HAPPEN

Isaiah 61:11

For as the earth bringeth forth her bud
    When winter is past,
The cold and temporal death are o'er
    And spring cometh at last,

As without fail, new life is raised
    Up unto perfection,
Making the world a much brighter place …
    Even so, will it happen.

For as the garden causeth things to grow
    That within are sown,
Naturally and oft' before
    Anyone has known,
Needless of human pow'r or skill
    The tiny seed will open,
To involuntarily yield fruit …
    Even so, will it happen.

Yes, even so will the Lord God cause
    Righteousness to spring forth,
And praise before all nations
    Will show its worth,
From within you and I will break out
    This seed in all directions,
As the earth and garden do bring forth …
    Even so, will it happen.

So worry not how it shall come
    But in the Lord, keep hoping,
For as surely as the earth brings forth …
    Even so, will it happen!

JUST LIKE MANY WATERS

SO WE, BEING MANY, ARE ONE BODY IN CHRIST,
AND EVERY ONE MEMBERS ONE OF ANOTHER.
—Romans 12:5

One Voice of many voices in the stream
    along the way …
The Voice of many waters John heard
    on the Lord's Day.
Beside the rushing stream, you pause
    and listen to the sound
That surges from the force of waters
    flowing o'er the ground;
And there, you think how every ripple's
    separate voice is drowned
By each of all the others', just like his
    to form one sound …

One voice of many voices in the stream
    along the way …
The Voice of many waters John heard
    on the Lord's Day.

Inside the Holy Spirit, John prayed
    and turned around;
Saw there One like the Son of man,
    and when He spoke, John found
His Voice as many waters, many peoples
    loud did sound.
Each one lost in the likeness of the
    Head that wore the crown.

One voice of many voices in the stream
    along the way …
The Voice of many waters John heard
    on the Lord's Day.

I KNOW HIM

FOR THE WHICH CAUSE I ALSO SUFFER THESE THINGS:
NEVERTHELESS I AM NOT ASHAMED: FOR I KNOW
WHOM I HAVE BELIEVED, AND AM PERSUADED
THAT HE IS ABLE TO KEEP THAT WHICH I HAVE
COMMITTED UNTO HIM AGAINST THAT DAY.
1 Timothy 1:12

I know Him …
        Fear doth flee.
I love Him and perfect love
Casts all fear far away from me.

I know Him …
        Not a church or creed,
But a true and living Savior
By Whom my soul is freed.

I know Him …
        His Goodness He gives
To me. For all my own is not enough
To make me live.

I know Him …
        I hold the only key
To Heaven's gates and perfect peace
For all eternity.

All else shall be shaken
        Shall fall and let me down;
But knowing Him, I know where'er
        I stand is solid ground.

COMFORT

6:00 A.M.

MY VOICE SHALT THOU HEAR IN THE MORNING,
O LORD; IN THE MORNING WILL I DIRECT MY
PRAYER UNTO THEE, AND WILL LOOK UP.
—Psalm 5:3

It's time to get up with the farmers.
It's time to get up with the birds.
It's time to get up with my Jesus.
It's time to get up with His Word.

It's time to get up and start praising
And down on my knees in prayer;
For I know that His sweet Holy Spirit
Is coming to meet me there.

It's time to get up to a new day,
And whatever awaits me ahead
I'll face without fear because He is near.
It's time to get up out of bed!

It's time to get up in a new way,
Renewed in my heart and my mind,
More in His likeness and image,
More in His life divine.

He knows just when I lie down
And He knows just when I arise;
And He knows that sometimes it's hard
To open these sleepy eyes.

So He sends along the sunshine
To brighten up the morn
And remind me of His Promise
To keep me safe and warm.

You know, I'll be satisfied on the day
When at last I get up to see …
My Lord and all of Heaven
Coming down to welcome me!

I SHALL BE SATISFIED, WHEN I AWAKE, WITH THY LIKENESS."
(Psalm 17:15)

TODODAY I LOVE YOU MORE

But when he was yet a great way off, his father saw him, and had
compassion, and ran, and fell on his neck, and kissed him.
Luke 15:20

The zeal I loved You with
back then …
        Thoughts told me …
'twould never end,
Howe'er, such feelings …
        did but begin …
           A voyage …
                unto the deep.

For since, I've dwelt …
        with weariness …
           Vanity and …
                selfishness,
Wandered much …
        in foolishness …
           Nearly lost my sight …
           and soul.

All those times You must …
        have known …
           My heart was heavy …
           as a stone;
If You had not …
        Your good love shown …
        I would have …
           surely perished!

The times I thought that …
        all was lost …
           I'd bought the wind …
              at Your love's cost …

My tender shoots …
 shrouded in frost …
  Howbeit, You stayed …
  by my side.

Oh, when I see that …
 all this while …
  You guarded me …
   as a soft, young child,
Led with chastisement …
 or with Your smile …
  And taught me …
   to love You more!

I can't contain …
 the fathomless rage …
  It draws me 'neath …
   Love's beckoning waves
That deepen, deepen …
 with the days …
  I Love …
   You More …

More I love than …
 e'er before …
  The One Who took me …
   from the shore …
And hast preserved my life …
 thus far …
  And will bring me …
   to the end.

More than a Friend …
 Beloved to me …
  More than all …
   You used to be,
What was hidden …
 You made me see …
  AND TODAY …
   I LOVE YOU MORE!

WHEN YOU DON'T UNDERSTAND

I DREW THEM WITH CORDS OF A MAN, WITH BANDS OF
LOVE: AND I WAS TO THEM AS THEY THAT TAKE OFF THE
YOKE ON THEIR JAWS, AND I LAID MEAT UNTO THEM.
—Hosea 11:4

There were some things I didn't understand.
    To Bunny, pet and friend, I turned aside
    And brought to her two leaves so green and wide.
The first I held to her with outstretched hand—
She eagerly received and thought it grand.
    Howe'er, the next I left upon my lap—
    Poor Bunny, then confused, thought some mishap,
Hopped about, and looked as to demand

Of me the thing that she so desired best.
'Til after seeking much she found it there
And in my arms she came to feed and rest,
    A deeper nearness with my heart to share …
I knew then why "not understanding" came—
For God used it to draw me just the same.

HAPPINESS

FOR I HAVE LEARNED, IN WHATSOEVER STATE
I AM, THEREWITH TO BE CONTENT.
—Philippians 4:11

Tho' of love
I oft' am looted,
Twice deceived,
And persecuted—
Tho' my heart
A place to tread
And leave bereft,
Uncomforted—
Counted out
Before I've tried,
Ill-accused,
Scorned … denied,
I greatly rejoice as on I go
For Jesus loves me this I know.

STARS

Twinkling candles … Held by angels …
    Wandering along the paths of night,
        Singing, "Peace to God's beloved children!"
        Sending happiness on rays of light.
Some are bright … Drawing nearer.
    Some are flickering … Still afar.
        But know, my friend, they are there to keep you
        To the ends of the earth wherever you are.

One shines in a bedroom window
    A precious child to see,
        And hovers near when it hears,
        "Lord, I pray Thy love guard me."
Another pours down blessed hope
    To a widow on her knees
        And there remains throughout the night
        To keep her company.

Across the land … Across the sky
    Others have found a thrill;
        And they rejoice as the believers below
        Give worship and praise from hearts in God's Will.
Now here, alone, I lie in my bed
    And see them all above;
        My heart is aware of His melting Presence
        Aware of consuming Love.

Throughout the night I have no fear …
    I remember what Jesus prayed,
        "Father, don't take them from the world,
        But keep them from the evil that slays."
Twinkling candles … Carried by angels
    Throughout this weary land,
        Reminding men to turn from sin
        And rest in the care of God's Hand.

THE GREATEST PROMISE

Happy I was.

> The sun shone warmth into my heart.
> Birds did sing the praises I
> > could not express.

Everywhere there was GOD rejoicing
> I saw His beauty in all things
> Overwhelming my soul and
> surpassing the capacity of its recesses.

I was sad.
> The sky overhead grew dark and cloudy.
> A barren chill was biting through the air.
> I lifted crying eyes up
> > to the heavens.

Then, there began a light rain.
> GOD'S tears fell upon my face
> and ran down my cheeks
> mingling with my own.

His Promise was true.
> "Always, I am with you."

LET US HOLD FAST THE PROFESSION OF OUR FAITH WITHOUT WAVERING; (FOR HE IS FAITHFUL THAT PROMISED). (Hebrews 10:23)

THE MOST WONDERFUL SOUND

LOVE SUFFERETH LONG, AND IS KIND; ENVIETH NOT,
VAUNTETH NOT ITSELF, IS NOT PUFFED UP, DOTH
NOT BEHAVE ITSELF UNSEEMLY, SEEKETH NOT HER
OWN, IS NOT EASILY PROVOKED, THINKETH NO EVIL;
REJOICETH NOT IN INIQUITY, BUT REJOICETH IN THE
TRUTH; BEARETH ALL THINGS, BELIEVETH ALL THINGS.
HOPETH ALL THINGS, ENDURETH ALL THINGS.
LOVE NEVER FAILETH.
—1 Corinthians 13:4–8

IT SOUNDS …

like the dripping of balm on a hurting soul
     a crackling fire 'midst deathly cold
     sweet music in the house of mourning
     to the darkest night, a bright new dawning.

like the trickle of rain on a drought-stricken land
     the jingle of coins in a hungry hand
     the resounding call to one lost and afraid
     a lullaby in the ears of a babe.

like peace proclaimed after the war
     the answerless finding a door
     mighty waves breaking on a rocky shore
     present-wrapping paper torn …

like a cleansing flow that washes clean
     the final cheer for a winning team
     life springing forth as the shell cracks apart
     old stones breaking, crumbling, releasing a heart …

The utterance … "I LOVE YOU."

AFTER THE RAIN

FOR WHOM THE LORD LOVETH HE CHASTENETH, AND
SCOURGETH EVERY SON WHOM HE RECEIVETH; IF YE
ENDURE CHASTENING, GOD DEALETH WITH YOU AS WITH
SONS … THAT WE MIGHT BE PARTAKERS OF HIS HOLINESS.
NOW NO CHASTENING FOR THE PRESENT SEEMETH TO
BE JOYOUS, BUT GRIEVOUS: NEVERTHELESS AFTERWARD
IT YIELDETH THE PEACEABLE FRUIT OF RIGHTEOUSNESS.
—Hebrews 12:6–7, 10–11

To make me as clean
as the leaves are green after the rain
You must oft' let me lie
in the weather and cry tears of pain—
Out 'neath the thick clouds
'midst thunderings loud and there feel
The torrents drown my foliage
trembling under the ravage without appeal—
Out in the great cold
where dampness enfolds me in the fog,
In the downpours imposed
to which I'm exposed in the sog.
But if I'd been hid
'neath a sheltering lid from the shower,
Darkness and dust
would overcrust my life and power;
And I could never sing
of the glistening drops that cling when the sun
                            shines again.
And I'd never be as clean
as the leaves are then so green
                 after the rain …

A LETTER TO HOME

FOR ALL FLESH IS AS GRASS, AND ALL THE GLORY OF
MAN AS THE FLOWER OF GRASS. THE GRASS WITHERETH
AND THE FLOWER THEREOF FALLETH AWAY.
—1 Peter 1:24

THEIR INWARD THOUGHT IS THAT THEIR HOUSES
SHALL CONTINUE FOR EVER, AND THEIR DWELLING
PLACES TO ALL GENERATIONS; NEVERTHELESS,
MAN BEING IN HONOUR ABIDETH NOT.
—Psalm 49:11–12

My Dear Old Home,

I'll write a line or two
    to make it known how oft' I think of you
At times it seems to be a bit unfair
    for neither car, nor boat, nor plane can take me there
The streets and lanes that used to lead the way
    are buried in the ruins of yesterday
The house and lawn are neither to be found
    New different things have filled their space of ground
The cheerful shops and folks I used to know
    I often wonder where they e'er did go
I look for Mom and Dad 'til I recall
    That Death doth come to claim the souls of all
The children who did run with me as friends
    will never run as children friends again
E'en the old oaks I look in vain to see
    the stumps not even left for memory
The gardens and the fields are covered o'er
    Lost as Atlantis fathoms from the shore
familiar sounds and voices heard ne'er more
    The only place my old home does yet lie
is in my heart and dreams
    and mind's eye.

ANOTHER LETTER TO HOME

WHEN I LAID THE FOUNDATIONS OF THE EARTH …
WHEN THE MORNING STARS SANG TOGETHER, AND
ALL THE SONS OF GOD SHOUTED FOR JOY?
—Job 38:4, 7

LORD, THOU HAST BEEN OUR DWELLING
PLACE IN ALL GENERATIONS.
—Psalm 90:1

ACCORDING AS HE HATH CHOSEN US IN HIM
BEFORE THE FOUNDATION OF THE WORLD.
—Ephesians 1:4

And so I think it best and truly wise
to turn my heart toward Home beyond the skies.
For after all, 'twas there I was conceived
and in the mind of God did first I breathe
before He formed my soul inside the babe
before the child to Mom and Dad He gave.
Sweet stories of my Home I dear recall
and pray that from its Promise I'll not fall.
I'm looking for a City made by God
a better Home than earthly feet have trod
A better Country that is heavenly
that God is not ashamed to prepare for me.
There the heav'n above and earth below
shall never change or pass away I know,
but for ages without end they shall remain

righteousness, peace, and joy shall dwell the same.
It is a Kingdom that cannot be moved;
It's where I'm from and where I'm going to.
A Holy City from which I'll ne'er depart
and separations rend my very heart
Where God dwells with His own
      and they with Him,
        where sorrow, death, and pain come to an end.
Made of gold and silver with walls of jasper stone
'Tis wonderful to think about my home!
The gates of pearl and streets transparent glass
that never decay ah, but for ever last!
A River there is flowing oh so clear
A tree of life that bears its fruit all year.
There's no more curse and we shall see His face.
The Lord Himself gives light to all the place!
And on that blessed mountain that's called Zion
I know the saints and elders are a'singing.
These are they who always followed Him;
These are they redeemed from among men.
"Great and marvelous are Thy works!" they sing
"Just and true Who shall not fear our King?
Nations every one to Thee shall come
and worship when Thy judgments all are done!"
And from the Spirit and the Bride I hear
A voice that is saying, "Let the sons of men draw near.
Come, let him that is athirst now come
To freely take the water of life now come."
No, my home is not lost and never shall be!
Each day more of its beauty I can see.

MY FRIEND

THIS IS MY BELOVED, AND THIS IS MY FRIEND,
O DAUGHTERS OF JERUSALEM.
—Song of Solomon 5:16

I have a Friend Who knows me well,
  Who's searched me through and through,
  Who sees each time that I sit down
  And when I rise up too,
  Who understands my very thoughts
  Before they come to mind,
  And cares for all the paths I walk
And places I lie down.

Not a word is on my tongue
  But He hears and knows it fully;
  With a hedge of love surrounds
  And guards behind, before me.
  If I ascend to heaven,
  He flies beside me there;
  If my bed is made in hell,
His Presence still I share.

If I take wings and go away
  To the loneliest place of the sea,
  Even there His Own right Hand
  Will follow to Hold and lead me,
  Such knowledge is too wonderful!
  So high … I can't attain,
  And Jesus's love forever more
That I can E'er explain!

IN ME

The Israelites faced with fear the Red Sea full before,
       Sending on waves its warnings
       Washing their hopes from the shore.
While I stood in another place just a short way past,
       Surrounded by uncertain ground
       Where shadows dark were cast.

HE rolled aside the waters of the mighty sea,
       Then He turned and said, "I'm going to lead you;
       Put your trust in ME!"

TO ME

WHAT HAVE I TO DO ANY MORE WITH IDOLS? I
HAVE HEARD HIM, AND OBSERVED, HIM.
—Hosea 14:8

Jesus is peace …
  He is safety
  He is rest
  and security … To me.

Jesus is joy …
  He is pleasure
  He is delight
  and happiness … To me.

Jesus is almighty …
  He is able
  He is willing
  and ready to save … To me.

Jesus is a refuge …
  He is defense
  He is protection
  and deliverance … To me.

Jesus is life and breath …
  He is health
  He is strength
  and power … To me.

Jesus is King …
  He is Lord
  He is sovereign
  and supreme … To me.

Jesus is bread …
  He is water
  He is all my needs
  and sufficiency … To me.

Jesus is real
  He is alive
  He is warmth
  and near … To me.

Jesus is success
  He is gain
  He is wealth
  and freedom … To me.

Jesus is wisdom
  He is knowledge
  He is truth
  and understanding … To me.

Jesus is love
  He is comfort
  He is care
  and always there … To me.

Jesus is everything
  He is infinite
  He is eternal
  and all that matters … To me.

How about you?

ALWAYS AND FOREVER

The white pine stands there,
as always … always green … never bare.
In the face of every hour …
never moving from its place.
I view its awesome sameness …
throughout the four seasons … In
winter snow … the boughs blow … and shake.

March and April … rains fall
around it … leaving it to stand alone
    … like a drenched, ragged beggar …
until the summer sun … shines the
warmth of love … on the same quivering
needles … And there bestows a
royal sheen.

I go … and come again … and the
white pine yet stands … When I lie down,
it continues to loll in the breeze.
I rise … during the night … In the
moonlight does it stand … 'til the dawning
of the day … the week … the month …
the year … The white pine stands there … Always.

May Christians' hearts stand there …
as always … always green … never bare.
In the face of every hour … never
moving from their place … Standing
in awesome fixedness … throughout
life's expanse.

Let winter's snow fail their
hearts to shake … In rains of pain
when they stand alone … let them stand.
Until the Son … HE will shine … upon
enduring hearts … and there bestow..
enduring love … enduring life …
enduring legacy of glory.

Let HIM go … and come again …
and let them yet stand … When they lie
down … their hearts awake … and in the
moonlight … stand … or in the darkness
of the new moon … Until the dawning
of the day … the week … the month …
the year … eternity!

May Christian hearts stand there … Forever.

REST

Rest, My child, now
All is well.
I love you more than words can tell.
Growing you are,
Perfect you'll be,
Living in safety ... Looking to Me.

THE LORD HATH APPEARED OF OLD UNTO ME, SAYING, "YEA, I HAVE LOVED THEE WITH AN EVERLASTING LOVE." (Jeremiah 31:3)

PRAYERS

MORNING PRAYER

O THOU THAT HEAREST PRAYER, UNTO
THEE SHALL ALL FLESH COME.
—Psalm 65:2

Lord, I need Thy strength to live this day,
I need Thy power that I may overcome,
I need Thine ability to help others,
And Thy grace to help myself.

I need Thy love, Lord, to do the right thing,
I need Thy mercy to govern my relationships,
I need Thy courage to stand by the Truth,
And the Truth to stand by me.

Lord, today, I need Thy meekness to well bear my cross,
Today, I need Thy joy that I may be strong,
I need Thy righteousness that I may Keep Thy Words;
Today, Lord, I need Thy life, not mine.

PARADOX

THIS IS A DAY OF TROUBLE, OF REBUKE, AND OF
BLASPHEMY: FOR THE CHILDREN ARE COME TO THE
BIRTH, AND THERE IS NOT STRENGTH TO BRING
FORTH WHEREFORE LIFT UP THY PRAYER FOR THE
REMNANT THAT IS LEFT.… THAT SHALL AGAIN TAKE
ROOT DOWNWARD AND BEAR FRUIT UPWARD.
—Isaiah 37:3–4, 31

It's the first day of spring, and snow's on the ground.
Ready for change but still making the rounds.
Lift up a prayer for the remnant today
To take root and bear fruit in a spiritual way.
Oh, can't you hear what I mean when I say?
"It is time to bring forth, but the strength is not found;
It's the first day of spring, and snow's on the ground."

MY DAILY BREAD

TREMBLE THOU EARTH, AT THE PRESENCE OF THE
LORD; WHICH TURNED THE ROCK INTO A STANDING
WATER, THE FLINT INTO A FOUNTAIN OF WATERS.
—Psalm 114:7–8

To greet You with the first breath of each morn
    To see Your face when first I open my eyes,
    And step into the heav'nlies when I rise
This is my sustenance and with which myself adorn.
To feel You within me each hour fresh born
    Bringing my ways ever unto Thy ways,
    Ever drawn unto Thy holy, high ways.
Daily purified as a sheep that is shorn.

Trembling at Thy Word as I lie down
    Whate'er of rock or stone has entered me
       Hardened crusts that form throughout the day
Are melted in the moment of the sound
    Your Presence brings, and there I see
       The flint becomes a fount of Heaven's spray!

FREE IN THEE

Oh, that my thoughts would of none but others think!
Would that my lips speak naught but of Thee!
Oh, that my heart would seek pursuit of Thy Kingdom alone!
For surpassing limitation, I'd then be wholly free!

I MUST

THEN SAID I, LO, I COME TO DO THY WILL, O GOD.
—Hebrews 10:7

After Calvary ... I will do ...
    anything ... to follow You ...
        Not only ... after Calvary,
            but after the Life ... You lived for me.

For YOUR Words, Lord ... I can hear ...
    alight in pain ... upon my ear,
        "I must suffer ... many things
            to give ... My loved children wings."

And death was not ... the only price ...
    but every day ... You gave Your life.
        In all things ... tempted, proved, tried,
            said, *"I must* ... be the Sacrifice.

"Perfect ... and without a spot ...
    I must ... be the Lamb of God,
        Or else God's plan ... may never be,
            My loved children ... Ne'er go free."

Thirty-three ... and one half years ...
    You bore this toilsome life ... down here.
        And all Your moments ... all Your way
            became a price ... You lived to pay.

My soul, you shall ... no longer sleep ...
    like those disciples ... three
        Who slumbered ... in the evening breeze,
            the Lord ... a'laboring on His knees.

My soul, can you ... not watch one hour?
    This mortal life ... is but a flower
        That withers ... in the noonday heat.
            Oh, watch, my soul ... at Jesus's feet!

For the servant … does not stand above …
    the Master; … you too must keep yourself in love.
        Poured out wine … for others' sake;
            Broken bread … to cease the ache …

Of hunger … in my brethren, Lord …
    for life and freedom … needs upstored.
        And how, Lord … will You fill their souls,
            lest I am yielded … clean and whole?

An empty vessel … flooded o'er …
    by You … alone opens the door.
        To my heart … You now entrust
            Your Giving … and *I must, I must, I must.*

DEAR GOD

BUT GOD WILL REDEEM MY SOUL FROM THE POWER
OF THE GRAVE: FOR HE SHALL RECEIVE ME.
—Psalm 49:15

Dear God, my soul must be … like the tender
    leaves that grow upon the tree … Born
    of Thee … so pure and clean … Maturing
    to Thy deep, dark green … There upon the
    tree of life a'hanging … Through the Spring
    of youth … there ever-changing … Through
    Summer's heat … and into Autumn's aging …
    … and Winter's death.

All the leaves … must one day fall … no matter
    how many be they all … Each one green
    will turn to brown … and a chilly breeze
    will send them down … Howe'er, they
    trust … their Father's plan … E'en though
    they have no hope … to rise again … How
    much more should I … Thy child and friend,
    … ever look to Thee?

For whether I fall in Spring … at the start;
    if March winds … blow my stem apart … Or
    Summer's drought doth leave me dry …
    and beneath the sun … I downward fly … Or
    shaken by the Autumn wind … I find myself
    a'falling then … Or whether Winter brings the end,
    … I'm hid with Thee.

It matters not … when or however … from the
    tree of this life I'm severed … For Thine
    eye upon me is true … Tho' I fall, and
    when I do … I'll fall into Thy vast eternity
    For there'll be no ground … below to
    receive me … *Only* Thine arms … where
    life is … and There … is Free.

THE WELL OF LIFE

AND THOU SHALT MAKE THEM DRINK OF THE RIVER OF
THY PLEASURES. FOR WITH THEE IS THE FOUNTAIN OF LIFE.
—Psalm 36:8–9

Thy mouth is a well of life unto me,
    Oh Lord.
At times, I would die, but streams
      from Thy lips are poured,
      Down to my fainting soul.

The drinkings that from Thy cistern
      all pure do flow
Into and clean through my being
      and there oft' endow
    Floods greater than I can bear.

So whether I sip at springs
      that ne'er run dry,
Or fathom the floods that flow
      from Thy fount on High,
      I cherish them all.

Yea, all that drop from Thine
      most precious tongue
And fall in the spray and foam that
      about are hung,
    And burst me forth unto the light!

IN THE PALM OF HIS HAND

To give Him my all and never a part
Is the cry of this, my heart.
    To walk with God from sun to sun
    Doing only and all He wills to be done.

All my desires, by Him designed
And brought to fulfillment in His good time.
    Bound to His side without cord or chain
    Unrivaled bonds, upon me lain.

Surrender without complaint or plea
Would rather die than be set free …
    Communicate continually.

Serving Him well, alone doth impel
My soul. Oh, one day I'll know and tell
    How thus serving Him, life is so grand …

Days without end in the palm of His Hand …
Days without end in the palm of His Hand.

THE TREE OF MY LIFE

LIKEWISE, RECKON YE ALSO YOURSELVES TO
BE DEAD INDEED UNTO SIN, BUT ALIVE UNTO
GOD THROUGH JESUS CHRIST OUR LORD.
—Romans 6:11

Let winter come …
        Making the bright leaves
        of myself … green and red
  … gold and flaming orange,
Fall from the tree of my life,
        dead and dry … and brown
        to the ground … never to
        rise or live again …
That the coming of spring …
        may applaud the birth of
        the fresh, tender leaves
        of the new creation …
        eternal and incorruptible …
  … which is Christ …
Bursting forth from the tree of my life!

FINAL PRAYER

Lord! You are mighty; You are strong …
Break through these clouds of doubt and wrong.
Break through the clouds that hide Your way.
Break through the night, and give me day!
Lord! Do not hide Your way behind
Uncertain shadows in my mind,
But show me Heaven that is Thine;

Show me how to make it mine
    'Til no hindrance at all remains
Flowing in me, out from me, are but Heaven's strains!

RHYMED NARRATIVES

TRUST

On the borderline edge between darkness and light
was the lonely place where I stood that night.
Up to this point, my path had been clear,
but now I looked ahead into a land of drear.
The light was fading; my heart began to pound.
Then I heard HIS voice. Oh, that sweet, familiar sound!
"My dove, look into that darkness and gloom
I've not left you; I've chosen this way for you
The way to my heart is that faintly glowing trail
Remember My strength is your strength, and you I'll not fail!"

Now with His love burning warm in my heart,
I began to tread that path through the dark
And upon that path, my eyes stayed true;
for if I dared look away, I'd have lost my view.
I wondered whatever could lay ahead
but I could not see, so I just believed what He'd said.
On into the forest Would I here be lost?
No! I must find HIS heart whatever the cost!
A little farther on then, I shuddered with fear,
    and when I cried, my Shepherd just didn't seem quite so near
For then I thought of "the spider."[1]*
I stopped for a moment and whispered a prayer,
"I trust You, My Father, I'm in Your care."
Another step I felt the "web" brush my face,
but I held to my righteousness as He filled me with faith.
"The 'web,' that's all; I'll walk right on.
HE won't let 'the spider' touch one of His Own."
I knew HE would cause me to overcome
but when I felt "the spider" crawling, I knew I was done.

The light of my path was now fainter than ever,
and I wondered if HE was watching to see my heart quiver.

The "spider" was crawling; I felt every move.

---

[1] * "The spider" here is metaphorically representative of one's great battle or trial in life.

My Master had called me, but now what should I do?
I waited, but the only answer I heard
was the silence, the love in my heart, and His Word.
Against HIS Will, I would not fight
when to my great shock, I felt the "spider" bite.
"My God!" I cried out in my pain.
(My tears began as did the rain.)
"You've been my hope, Lord, from the start.
I've trusted You with all my heart.
I've tried never to question Your divine plan,
for You promised to cover me with Your hand.
But now it seems You've long been gone.
All my seeking seems vain and terribly wrong.
I've come so far and still You're not here.
Instead, my soul has been swallowed in fear."
I thought surely HE must come to me then,
but rather I grew numb as the venom flowed within.
HE said He would never disregard my plea,
but the glowing path I could no longer see.

I saw nothing. Oh, but what did I hear?
A roar from above split the atmosphere!
The scream of an eagle, a heart-cry for freedom,
and HE in righteousness adorned with His Kingdom!
His voice was all love, victorious and holy.
Then, unrestrained, that same cry arose within me
and with strength I never knew I had,
I cried like the eagle, "HE hath made me glad!"
A force like the power of a raging sea
caused the careless things of my dark path to flee.
Perfect love cast out my fear.
Jesus and I were ruling here.
HIS language I could understand.
HE is the Perfect One and Grand!
And as I looked on HIM, I saw myself reflected—
what wonder! In Him, I am perfected!
The words of love, I could not say,
but His eyes tell He is well pleased today.
Those times He knew when I could not see,
but He never once departed from me.
Now the very air I breathe is the wind of love

and at last I'm HIS own beloved dove.
He desired my *trust* more than songs in the night,
My obedience more than sacrifice.
HE says, "I've counted each trying step you've trod.
Now how do you like the heart of God?"
Then as worship flowed from me unto my King,
I heard the angels start to sing.

(WHO IS THIS COMING UP FROM THE WILDERNESS, LEANING
UPON HER BELOVED? ….FOR LOVE IS STRONG AS DEATH ….AND
MANY WATERS CANNOT QUENCH LOVE…. NOW HAS HE BROUGHT
ME INTO HIS BANQUETING HOUSE AND HIS BANNER OVER ME
IS LOVE.) --- Song of Solomon 8:5–7, 2:4

WHY WILL YOU DO THIS?
HAVEN'T YOU BEEN TOLD …
YOU'LL LIVE FOREVER
AND YOU WON'T GROW OLD? …

WOE TO THEM THAT ARE AT EASE IN ZION … IF THEY HAD
STOOD IN MY COUNSEL, AND HAD CAUSED MY PEOPLE TO HEAR
MY WORDS, THEN THEY SHOULD HAVE TURNED THEM FROM
THEIR EVIL WAY. (Amos 6:1, Jeremiah 23:22)

This world is falling fast away … Why waste
your shortened days in play? Millions are
dying in wicked sin … not knowing how to enter
in … Why do your foolish hearts grow dim?
Your eyes no longer are beholding Him … Your
light of love is growing cold … as you feast
and make merry with the rest of the world …
You eat your meat and jingle your gold, while
the Lord's sheep are dying right in the fold!
Your flesh is filled and your laughter rings
high … blaring out the withering spirit's cry.
My people … so bound … Will you never be free
to walk in My glorious liberty? Why walk your
own ways … refusing to see … when you could
be here in the heavenlies with Me?
My coming is soon as you will see … but I
wonder if you'll even be aware of Me. When

I return with a shout … will your ears hear
or be filled with this world that you hold
so dear? Will your eyes behold Me … Your
Reigning King? Will you love Me then? Will
I make your hearts sing? … Or will you
be blinded by your restless affairs … too
carnally minded My glory to share? Would
you love "self" more than the Beginning and
End? Would you love pleasure more than your
Almighty Friend? … Seek Me, My people,
for I'm not far away … Why increase the
distance … day after day? …
As the beast cares not for man's pleasure or
power … but lives and enjoys his vile ways
every hour … So My people still end every
day far below … Never seeking the true
and the highest to know …
I'm offering you the life and realm of Christ;
It's paid for with a bloody price … Why
will you cling to the vain cares that bind …
when I'm calling you to partake of my mind?
All of your joy … and that you do … in a
moment's time could all be through … and a
world of others after you … will live and die
in this pattern too … Awake! My lambs,
I'm leading on! Be not deceived by the fool's
careless song … Your limited world will
vanish as naught; but some will see what a
Good Thing I've wrought! … Oh Come, My
Redeemed, My Sought-out Ones! Forsake your
ways … and follow the Son … Let Me not return
to your lowly mirth … Oh let My eyes find
faith on the earth! …
Why tarry so long … in ignorant style? Look
up to escape the tempter's wiles … Why be
like your fathers … that stubborn lot? So
often I would have loved you … but ye would not!

ALL THE KING'S MEN

BLESSED ARE THEY THAT DO HIS COMMANDMENTS,
THAT THEY MAY HAVE RIGHT TO THE TREE OF LIFE, AND
MAY ENTER IN THROUGH THE GATES INTO THE CITY.
—Revelation 22:14

In our times, there lived a Lord,
just and noble, Who ruled with love
and mercy. Powerful was His sword,
and mighty His hand to deliver was.
All His men were famed and blessed;
His gifts to them brought joy and peace.
As kinsmen were they fed and dressed.
So proud to be their Shepherd's sheep
until those two foul fiends heard
the news that made them envious.
They had no hearts, their name an unclean word.
The one was Sin, the other Fleshly Lust.
Both were set on men's fall and destruction,
loving to see them falter pitiless
enraged that there should come a One
to be their help, to save them from distress.
Thus, the two awaited the night
scheming plans of hate and doom,
exhilarant at thoughts of the bloody fight,
waiting to seal some poor man's tomb.
Then as darkness fell and grew heavy

and thick, the fiends did spread
their ugly wings, sharp and scaly,
And flew to where the men lay in their beds.
However, the Lord Who was all wise
was also watchful and saw them
afar off and called His men to rise,
to give their ear to Him.
"Awake!" He cried. "And shake yourselves
from sleep that has made you dull!
Come near and take your weapons from the shelves
where they've lain by, and bring oil
to give us light. For they have come
to war and take your bodies for a spoil."
So all arose and made a stand
as those two evil ones came near, screaming
horribly through the air, so as to incite fear,
then swooped down on the fortress there.
The men though shaken were brave
and sent their arrows swift
and sure, which made the fiends rave
that the good Lord such warriors kept.
So with the fierceness of a storm
that leaves none in its path,
they gathered all their power to harm
and rushed as never any hath …
which proved to be a dreadful blow
that brought down those protecting walls
that had been built by Him
Who was the Strength of men and their King …
With that, many fled out into the dark wind …

Yet there stood a few valiant of them to sing
the praises of their Lord's past victories
as those two evils fell on them hard
again and brought them to their knees.
In fire and smoke, these fled to their Lord,
Who rejoiced to find on earth such faith
and gird Himself with righteousness.
With the voice of triumph, He saith,
"Take heart, My young, fighting nobles,
for you will possess the land."

Then up He took to meet the foes
and fight them hand to hand.
But when they saw His countenance,
their inner parts of evil did fail;
For the light that shone from His glance
alone … made their terribleness seem frail.
Those heinous beasts set off to fly
for safety in their den;
But they were to never again soar high,
for the mighty Lord ripped off their pinions!
So they turned on foot like men
to run for their worthless lives;
but the Lord of valor was unwilling then
to let them depart in their wicked device
without vengeance for His faithful friends.
So with speed that words can't tell,
He chased those brutes to this earth's end,
And there He cast them down to Hell!

Then He returned and drew them 'round
whose trust in Him was true
and spread their names throughout the bounds
of that land unto the blue.
"My friends," quoth He in loving power,
"This night has proved you to Me well.
With victory we behold the morning hour
and My love for you, I will tell.
My servants you will no longer be;
from henceforth you will be known
as My sons, for this day I can see
within you a seed, growing strong
of My Own image, spirit, and blood;
and so this morn, I make you heirs and partakers
of My flood of wealth forever to share.
But as for those deserting fools
who fled for safety in the world,
leaving their Lord and comrades too,
let them to their fate be hurled.
May they ever wander all alone
as long as they can make their way
without a Lord to call them His own;

Through wandering, let them pay.
And, furthermore, My sons, to you
Let this be your constant reminder;
To fight to win among My chosen few,
Or else, hopelessly, to wander.

FROM THE AEOLIAN HARP

THE TRUE WORSHIPERS SHALL WORSHIP THE
FATHER IN SPIRIT AND IN TRUTH: FOR THE
FATHER SEEKETH SUCH TO WORSHIP HIM.
—John 4:23

THAT THEY SHOULD SEEK THE LORD, IF HAPLY
THEY MIGHT FEEL AFTER HIM, AND FIND HIM,
THOUGH HE BE NOT FAR FROM EVERY ONE OF US.
—Acts 17:27

Oh, the strains that are unleashed!
Songs of love … love unknown …
Songs of seeds just newly sown …
Songs of life … untasted yet …
Of power … strength to free … unfret!
On and on in endless rhyme
Tunes continue and expand,
Over and over and o'er again
Under influence of wide-open wind,
Vibrating sounds of communion with Him.
Oh, give to lips and tongues that voice!
That excel all mortal ability
That ring into eternity …
Throughout the realms of glory sought—
Rush of wings and water and thought.
Untaught … unlearned … unspeakable

Expressions of experience
At the height of life existence …
Wind and strings to form a whole—
Creator and creature releasing one soul!
That faints away with the onward sound
Into a dream that is so real …
That stops the thought and lets one feel
The life that lies ahead … beyond
The things known here beneath the sun.

Then, awaking … gradual … slow …
The sound resounding deep within,
Having searched the farthest end
Of all that is and makes a man
And having filled it all; oh, then …
Does throb throughout the entire soul
As it awakes so peacefully
Into an hour of serenity—
The hour before the evening falls
To lay in silence, great and small.

An hour where the chorus blend
Condescends into a hum
Reminiscent of the song
Occasionally ascending to its former height
Or fading into cessation … only to relight …
And rekindle … and reburn
The mellow hum that cannot cease.
Unconsciously … almost it seems
To flow … responding to the breeze
And to all it's heard and seen.
A new and penetrating sound …
United, grafted, in the heart
As one with God and wind, it starts—
A single strain that blends in one
All that has afore been done.
The echo of a mature relationship
With the Spirit that has played upon the soul,
As the wind upon the yielding strings did blow.
Of a tasting of a better land and love
And hearing mysteries just known above!

Of God so close, He ravishes the heart,
And makes the fire of earth a tiny spark
That is consumed in heavenly rays of bliss—
The mind and heart are transformed like to His.
A sound that stands as if alone,
With strength that has been full outpoured,
In reaching up to Heaven's door;
And there in weakness, findeth might
And hath lain hold upon the light!

And finally, it bursts once more
And rips the strings in a surge of praise …
Uncontrollably into a rage
Of joy … because the being is set free
Before the hush … when He gives His beloved sleep.

And even then, 'tis not all still;
For there … the stringed lips do quiver
Each time the Presence passes nearer,
And utter love songs through the air—
And in their sleep, yet whisper His care.

THE OUTCASTS

O GOD, THINE ENEMIES ROAR IN THE MIDST OF THY
CONGREGATIONS: THY SANCTUARY, THEY HAVE DEFILED
BY CASTING DOWN THE DWELLING PLACE OF THY NAME
TO THE GROUND … O DELIVER NOT THE SOUL OF THY
TURTLEDOVE UNTO THE MULTITUDE OF THE WICKED:
FORGET NOT THE CONGREGATION OF THY POOR FOREVER.
—Psalm 74:4, 7, 19

LO, I WILL SAVE THEE FROM AFAR, AND NONE SHALL
MAKE THEE AFRAID … AND OUT OF THEM SHALL
PROCEED THE VOICE OF THEM THAT MAKE MERRY: AND
I WILL MULTIPLY THEM AND GLORIFY THEM, AND THEY
SHALL NOT BE SMALL. THEIR CHILDREN ALSO SHALL BE
AS AFORETIME, AND THEIR CONGREGATION SHALL BE
ESTABLISHED BEFORE ME … FOR I WILL RESTORE HEALTH
UNTO THEE, AND I WILL HEAL THY WOUNDS, SAITH
THE LORD; BECAUSE THEY CALLED THEE <u>AN OUTCAST</u>,
SAYING, "THIS IS ZION, WHOM NO MAN SEEKETH AFTER."
—Jeremiah 30:10, 17–20

Listen, my friend, and you will hear … a rousing cry
from far and near … like the sound of a trumpet … a
hurricane gale … This cry from the heart does not falter
or fail. The voices are few, but the shout is strong;
The dark's closing in, and they haven't got long.
Through the rain … through the storm … through the hail

... and the night ... their eyes never fall from that small beam of light. Though reviled by men ... they stick to the fight ... and above all else ... keep their Master in sight. Religion derides them ... they are mocked by their brothers ... but for Christ, these have left even father and mother. Money ... gain ... fame ... friends ... none of these are important to them ... With Jesus as their Commander-in-Chief ... Heaven their goal ... and souls their Plea, they fight for God's Presence back in the temple, "Awake! thou slothful ... Be wise, oh simple!" As Proverbs says ... they cry in the streets ... when the churches won't have them ... as they've fallen asleep! ... Their eyes are blinded ... they won't hear the Truth ... but the fruit of their message is shown through the youth.

Yea, God's people are bold ... and for better or worse ... they fearlessly warn this sleeping Church. Their tongues are like swords ... their words like fire ... and their roar for Revival grows higher and higher! Their song of victory is giving them power ... to overcome the stinging blows of this hour ...

Their realm of high praise ... adoration ... and worship ... throws some in a spin ... and brings the world ... hot conviction. Of course, the religious are counteracting with a big sign for Revival ... or is it a series of meetings? ... when they say they love God, but they don't love their neighbor; when they rejoice in the Lord, but that joy seems to waver. They pray, but their voices are like tinkling brass ... the lips run free while the heart's in a cast ... Their sacrifice of praise is an abomination to God ... and He rules over them with an iron-made rod ... They glory in the acts but don't know the Actor ... strive for the creation but run from the Creator. They refuse to consecrate their lives to the Savior but fit in and indulge in immoral behavior. God requires of His Army ... a separated heart, but these have learned well of the counterfeit part. To the sinner ... their lives provide no example, but the Name of Jesus ... in the dust ... do they trample. Pride, which God hates ... is the theme of their lives ... as they trip their poor brother with gossip and lies. The time on their knees is now time with TV ... Rejecting

the warnings … lukewarm they will be! Miserable …
wretched … naked … and blind … They can't see it's
themselves who are falling behind.
The time is near … and though they think they are right,
Christ will come upon them like a thief in the night! …
to cast down every mountain … make every hill low … And
as the forerunners … God's children they go …
The heat of the fire has made them pure … The heat of the
Battle has prepared them for war! They are scattered
but God has promised to bring them together … as they
go out to preach and unfold revelation. Some faces may
resemble ice or flint … but this doesn't faze God's
"called out" one bit … They know time is short, and
the Church still slumbers … Christians grow cold,
and the sinner still blunders! So they preach all the
harder and exert every effort … go anywhere folks will
come together … The burden for souls and Revival is so
heavy … they leave streets and lanes for the highways and
hedges … Like John the Baptist … they call all to
repent … crying out at home … on the job … in a tent …
raising their voices in this world of dry bones … In the
midst of the wilderness … with all life packed and gone!
Like the prophets … Jeremiah and Isaiah … God's spokesmen
are telling the Church to stop playing.
COMMANDING Egypt and the bondage of Pharaoh … to turn
loose of the Church and let God's people go … Tho'
they shake down Babylon … and war against sin … the
love in this body … reaches deep within … When one
member hurts … the whole body feels pain. And when one
profits … all rejoice in the gain. Dissension has not
a chance among this people … so united … who find strength
in each other when trouble is sighted. The cords
binding like spirits … can never be broken … and God
sends them His Love as a unity token. Forward they march,
in one accord … with hearts and minds focused on
Jesus their Lord … With the whole armor of God, they
face every foe … making more progress than they'll
ever know! Tho' the counterfeits show off a sarcastic
front … they cower inside … and tremble at this bunch.
Just the sight of them … with such power within …
withholding nothing … pointing out hidden sin … Though

small and scattered, this chosen lot … possesses
something real that others have not. They stand tall
and strong as the world starts to sway … with the
confusion … turmoil … and deceit of this day …
Now the story has changed … and they're looking at you.
Thumbs up or down? What are you going to do? … The
eagle soars … the chicken scratches … Do you have on
your wedding garment … or rags and patches? God's
calling you out to bring you in … Forget the hurt and
the places you've been. Just seek after God … and all
that He is … Strive to be like Him … find His perfect
WILL … Erase every worry … fear … and doubt! Start
out right with a joyful shout! His life is your life …
and that is eternal … That's a reason to shout and
then preach with a fervor! Please don't turn your key
now and step on the gas … but brandish your
sword and join God's Outcasts!

BECAUSE THEY RECEIVED NOT THE LOVE OF THE TRUTH
THAT THEY MIGHT BE SAVED… GOD SHALL SEND THEM
STRONG DELUSION THAT THEY SHOULD BELIEVE A LIE…
AND BE DAMNED WHO BELIEVED NOT THE TRUTH BUT HAD
PLEASURE IN UNRIGHTEOUSNESS. BUT WE ARE BOUND TO
GIVE THANKS ALWAYS TO GOD FOR YOU, BRETHREN BELOVED
OF THE LORD, BECAUSE GOD HATH FROM THE BEGINNING
CHOSEN YOU TO SALVATION THROUGH SANCTIFICATION OF
THE SPIRIT AND BELIEF OF THE TRUTH: WHEREUNTO HE
CALLED YOU BY OUR GOSPEL TO THE OBTAINING OF THE
GLORY OF OUR LORD JESUS CHRIST. (II Thessalonians 2:9–14)

ODE TO THE BRIDE

AND THERE CAME UNTO ME ONE, SAYING, 'COME HITHER,
I WILL SHEW THEE THE BRIDE, THE LAMB'S WIFE. AND
HE CARRIED ME AWAY IN THE SPIRIT, AND SHEWED ME
THAT GREAT CITY … HAVING THE GLORY OF GOD, AND
HER LIGHT WAS LIKE UNTO A STONE MOST PRECIOUS,
EVEN LIKE A JASPER STONE, CLEAR AS CRYSTAL.
—Revelation 21:9–11

See the Maiden standing there … Unto her
Well beloved, fair … Though her mother's
children burn with ire … Because they understand
not her desire … To part with patriarchal
paths … To feed and rest with His Own flock …
Yet unburdened by their scornful wrath … She
waits upon and yields to His lovelock.

Oh, wonder at her watchfulness! … Call not
her waiting idleness! … Is it hard for you to
thus define … Her words "I charge you by the
roes and hinds … Do not stir up my love until
He please … Or bid me move when I've not heard
His voice … For they go not in haste who true
believe … I listen for 'Rise up and come' by
choice"?

Yet ye know by heart the tale … Of soldier
fighting in the vale … With valiant soul he
stands his ground … Tho' Death and horrors
close in round … For yet no word hath pierced

his ear … From Captain's lips Who seeth all …
And knoweth best in battles drear … When
"advance" or "retreat" to call.

Even so the Shepherd's tongue … Will in
perfect time say, "Come … Winter rain is over.
gone, and past. Birds and flowers fill the
earth at last … Thy hour of fruitfulness is
nigh at hand … The trees put forth green figs
and tender grapes … And soon will make a garden
of thy land … Where I may enter with delight
of taste."

It is unaccountable … That having made
her comfortable … The maiden rises up at once
and leaves … The warm, familiar things that
bring her ease … For she hath well perceived her
Loved One's knock … And goes about a'yearning
in the streets … Seeking Him at every city block …

'Til she finds and falls and worships at
HIS feet.

Have you never heard, my friend? … How
Mohammad sought to ken … The pure Arabians
among his steeds … Did all of them up yonder
mountain lead … Corralled there in the face of
burning sun … Corralled from mocking waters way
below … With much time passed, he let them
loose to run … At once to race with panting
hearts, to go.

A common thirst they sought to quench …
With one desire their bodies flinched … However,
at Mohammad's trumpet sound … The Arabians
alone did turn them 'round … And let the others
run ahead to drown the fire … Of drought within
their frames that forced on … Alone did these
forsake their lust, tho' dire … Relentlessly,
to heed the bugle tone.

'Twas theirs but noble instinct … 'Twas
hers the power to think … And act upon her
humble adoration … Of the Chiefest One among
ten thousand … Pow'r to let companions run
ahead … Pursuing loves to quench their fleeting
dreams … Pow'r to see His path a privileged

tread … Tho’ leading far from her own hopeful schemes.

Therefore will her King stand true … And with words of wisdom, woo … “My dove, My undefiled, is only one … Of her mother, there is other none … Fair as the moon or so clear as the sun (Son) … That looketh forth as holy, morning light … And offereth such a pure and sweet oblation … Return, return, return, oh Shulamite!”

She’d be joined to Jesus sure … And Jesus would be joined to her … Life is but to her continuation … Of His on earth, a life of separation … From goals, herself, to glorify … And vain attempts to be called great … For things that are esteemed by men as high … Are but the foolish things that God doth hate.

For even Jesus, Firstborn Son … If she’s to do as He has done … Walked with heart that sought not anything … Whereby the people would His praises sing … Nothing worthy of human laud … Or promotion in their eyes … And no pursuit to bring His Name applaud … But to glorify the Father, gave Himself a Sacrifice.

Of earth’s leaven, emptied now … The maiden stands on Heaven’s brow … The King is held within her galleries … The finite steps into eternity … One heart, one mind, even one purpose, blessed! … That which from the first God hath ordained … The two have merged into one happy rest … The Lord and she whom His Hand hath redeemed!